A
Young Man's Guide
to the Real World

QUOTES

"This is the best numb-butt, dead-leg, help me off
the toilet book ever"
—*The Author*

"This book will never be part of The Oprah Book Club"
—*Authors Wife*

"This book will not win a Pulitzer prize"
—*Authors Buddy who can barely read*

"This Author should definitely visit with
a qualified psychiatrist"
—*Just about everyone the author knows*

"This book needs to be read by as many people
as soon as possible"
—*Authors IRS Investigator*

"This book is a conservationist dream—read and
wipe—read and wipe"
—*Authors Tree Hugging Friends*

"What a piece of literary crap"
—*Authors Former Friend*

A
Young Man's Guide
to the Real World

Richard H. Eads

To order additional copies of this book, contact:
Xlibris Corporation
1-888-795-4274
www.Xlibris.com
Orders@Xlibris.com
42845

ACKNOWLEDGEMENT

I want to take a minute to thank some folks. I have been told by a reliable and expensive bottom feeder (lawyer) that as long as I don't mention their surnames (last names you idiots) and that I ask for their permission I'm not going to get my ass sued.

Deep breath—first off, I want to thank Mama (my wife) for listening to my rants about this book while taking great pains NOT to read it. I want to thank Jenbo for permission to use a picture of her butt-zee—Fun Bobby didn't have any say and his ass was too hairy anyway. I want to thank sub-genius Kirk for taking the time to read my work but more importantly for giving it to Holly who took his pragmatic and constructive criticism and made it funny. Jock for doing nothing more than laughing so if the book bombs it's his fault for making me think it was brilliant. Dobbin for the 10,000 foot suggestions because he knew I would tell him to fuck-off if he got too specific. Tara for being the only princess to read it and give me "two" big thumbs up with a promise to kick me in the balls the next time we get together. Thanks to Jay for telling me to remove some of the gratuitous F-Bombs—Fuck off Jay. Thanks to the poor bastards who tried to help me get to this point. Someone had to read this shit to lay it out. I am for sure going to hell. Thanks to Doctor Phil for convincing me that young people need tangible help and advice not fluffy bull shit from someone who has never been in a bar brawl or jumped on the ugly grenade for a friend. To the really hard-ass bastards who thought I was funny instead of kicking my ass. Thank you. And to the not so hard-ass bastards who allowed me to kick theirs. Thanks to the nameless friends and acquaintances and their bit parts in my life's experiences from the local council workers and their copious amounts of naughty magazines who helped me learn how to wank in sub zero temperatures to all those fat chicks who convinced me that I was "the" crusader for the "Fat Chicks Need Sex As Well" campaign. Genuine thanks to all the good looking nutcases who did the best they could to fuck with my head—bite me—and I hope your asses and tits finally defied gravity.

Last but not least my two boys who between them, in their own unique way, show me what a complete and utter nightmare I must have been at their age. I love you boys and before I will die I promise I will write another book about all the funny shit you have taught me. Please Enjoy . . . R H E

CONTENTS

PROLOGUE

(I Think That's What They Call An Introduction)

Self-help this and self-help that is all we seem to hear nowadays. How about a little sit-down chat with an old friend who can reflect on his life and give you some good old-fashioned advice. Many of us look back on our lives and say, "What if." In many cases, that reflection is based upon the illusions of grandeur that we get when we get older. If only I took that piece of advice, if only I caught that pass, if only I invested that money and if only I hadn't passed out and puked on her and a few thousand other "what ifs." Many of those "what ifs" could be translated into "What a fucking idiot I was."

What follows here is more along the lines of "look out," "beware," and if you can recognize *it,* then maybe you can avoid *it* or change the outcome. There are many lessons to be learned in our short time on this planet. However, very few (hetro) young men sit down and read self-help books, visit the local psychiatrist, or seek their parents' advice on key "growth" issues.

So this book is here to help you survive (and I do not use that word lightly) your younger years. Maybe after reading this book, you may avoid that butt kicking that is inevitably heading your way. Maybe you will be able to leave a casino with some money instead of a hangover, a sore dick, and empty pockets. Maybe you will get the hot chick for more than a two-second "excuse me" and maybe—just maybe—this book might help you think about events in a different light before they happen (ideal) or after they happen so they don't happen again.

For me, your author, I am in that phase of my life where I am still crazy enough to act and think like a twenty-five-year-old while being fifty. It is good to "still be crazy after all these years" without the inbred pitfalls that I had twenty-five years ago.

Just so you know (not that I give a shit) if I make a few bucks that I am not here to preach, be "holier than thou," judge, or condemn, but I am here to advise, coach, and educate.

The bottom line is if your younger years can be a little less bumpy for reading this book, then yah-fucking-hoo.

THE DICKHEAD THAT
IS WRITING THIS CRAP

In summary—you'll be glad to know—so you can maybe relate to your own life.

No real parents to speak of—bummer.

Raised in a children's home—another bummer.

Biggest crybaby going—I try hard to stop that from happening to my boys.

Recipient of quality grade A bullying—Note, Until Age twelve, when I pummeled the fuck out of KLL. My boys will not be bullied. Trust me.

Left school, didn't take a single exam, and ran away from home as soon as and as often as, possible—awesome.

Joined the Military—Stressful for sure, for a naïve sixteen-year-old.

Toughened up. Found discipline, rugby, boxing, fighting, drinking, and fucking—all in one go.

Had a diverse career—Say no more.

Traveled the world—Everyone *must* travel.

Moved to the good old US of A—glad to see the back of what was left of Great Britain.

Had six years of fun and hell all rolled into one—Mainly hell, but educational just the same.

Finally met a great woman (after plenty of quality attempts) who put up with my shit.

Calmed down a little—well, kind of. ☺

Had kids and got married. Calmed down a little more—well, kind of. ☺

Hit forty-five and realized, Jesus, I need to really calm it down a notch. ☹

Now FIFTY and spending two to three weekends a year acting like a twenty-five-year-old with old mates.

Active social life with ancient peers all year round-thrown in.

"Damn, when you summarize it like that, it doesn't seem like much, does it? The thing is, during the first half of my life, a lot of stuff happened. Some good, some bad, but rest assured, *all* educational."

CHAPTERS

Some of these chapters will be longer than others for the simple reason that I have more experience in some than in others. I will go through them in order of expertise and content, not importance. As you read, you can fill in the blanks, and each time you say, "I know what he means," "I saw that happen," "shit, I nearly did that," or "Yep, been there, seen it, and done it," send my publisher—oops me—$10.

1. DRINKING

2. FIGHTING

3. FUCKING

4. GAMBLING

5. CONFIDENCE

6. THE LAW

7. ILLEGAL DRUGS

8. RELIGION

CHAPTER 1

DRINKING

al·co·hol·ism

Function: *noun*

Date: 1860—more like early BC if you believe the history books

1: continued excessive or compulsive use of alcoholic drinks
2: poisoning by alcohol; *especially* : a complex chronic psychological and nutritional disorder associated with excessive and usually compulsive drinking

---

Alcoholic—hmm, interesting term unless of course you are a legitimate alcoholic who will think nothing of chugging a fifth of whiskey for breakfast. I want to focus on you "wannabe alcoholics." I read a definition of an alcoholic once and it stated that an alcoholic is a person who has three or more beers a day. Well, sign me the fuck up. In fact, you can sign up the whole of the British Royal Navy as the government gives everyone a daily ration of three cans of beer when they are on board a ship.

The point is, technically, many of you are "alchies" whether you recognize it or not. Think to yourself, Have I missed any days of work because I was too hung over?

Have I blacked out and not remembered what the hell happened the night before? Have I slept in a hedge and woke up to see "normal" people walking by on their way to lunch? Have you ever fucked a woman so ugly that you chewed off the arm she was lying on to get away and when you got home, you chewed off the other arm in case she was out looking for a one-armed man? Well, you get the idea, and I am sure that you can come up with some others.

Such as have you ever done something so stupid that, except for the fate of the gods, you would be dead now? Gives you cause for thought, doesn't it? I can think of eight for me, but how about just this one.

I once jumped off a bridge into a river, not too high, maybe forty feet. Funny as fuck at the time. Got picked up by the harbor police, was told I was a bad boy, and sent on my way. I was a legend with the boys for about two weeks.

Why only two weeks? Well, two weeks, later another "mini me," who was a little tiddly, did the same thing. He could swim like a fish, but the problem was that the man in the sky was in a bad mood and moved the tide out. Our young "Legend-to-Be" went in about ten feet of water, then plowed into the riverbed, just far enough where he couldn't free himself. Bye-bye, young man, see ya in the bar upstairs.

Now I know we can all get run over by a bus or get hit by lightning any time, any day, and anywhere. But we do not need to help it along. Playing chicken with cars, walking in bad neighborhoods at three in the morning, taking on multiple people in brawls, fake knife fights with real knives, and on and on can shorten the odds of getting to your twilight years. And I know you will find this hard to believe, but I bet you would never do any of these things stone cold sober.

There are many things that we can do when partying up a storm to save us and others a lot of grief. With many young people, or old farts for that matter, it is not always how much you drink but what you drink, how you drink it, your frame of mind when you drink, and the environment you drink in.

Let's look at the key parts of a good night on the piss.

What You Drink

We all have drinks that we like, those are fine, but you must watch out for and recognize that we all have a demon drink. What the fuck is a demon drink, you may well ask. A demon drink is the one drink that turns you into a complete and utter asshole. Me, it was whiskey. Drank whiskey, got violent, and found I was good at knocking people around.

It wasn't until I got arrested five or six times in eighteen months that I put two and two together. Haven't touched a drop of whiskey in thirty years. Now just because I haven't had whiskey in a while it doesn't mean that other factors (along with a suitable stand-in demon drink) haven't turned me into a supernova asshole on occasion.

So how about this: think about the time you nearly or did get in a fight with your best mate. Think about the last time you called your girlfriend or wife a bitch. Think about the last time when you were thinking, "I can kick that biker with the thirty-six-inch bicep's ass."

And think about the last time you drove home and found your car up on the curb. See if there is a common drink in those events and stay the hell away from it—that is your demon drink.

Now, if you are a complete and utter asshole 24/7 anyway, then fuck it, drink anything not nailed down.

How You Drink

I am sure that you all know the basics. Never drink on an empty stomach and drink a LOT of water either during or after a good session. Don't mix your drinks (well, not too much).

It's okay to go from beer to shorts (*shots*) but try not to sample every cocktail known to man in one sitting. Cocktails are like people, some just do not mix well with others.

Shots, you've got to love 'em and hate them at the same time. They are the kiss of death for a good night out. You are cruising along, having a great time on your fifth beer, talking to a babe (intelligently), and some bright spark says, "Hey, who wants a shot?" Turn around, look them in the eyes and say, "Not me."

Of course, we know that you won't/can't do that because then you would be "pussy boy" and that just wouldn't do. So here's what you do. You pick a shot that is not going to absolutely fuck you up and send you to Mars. Again, drink selection is the key. Your mates, who are also doing a shot, will not think you are a "pussy boy" as long as you do a shot. Pick one that is not as deadly as a Vulcan Mind Meld, for example. Who gives a fuck what they want, pick the furthest shot type from your demon drink and sup up.

Do not feel obligated to immediately buy the next round of shots. If anything, encourage another round of beers to dilute the shot that is churning your stomach and fucking with your brain cells as you speak.

Oh, and by the way, if the girls want shots, good for them. Hell, stud, you can even buy them. *But*, and it is a big *but*, if you are planning to "get some," stop them before they get to shot number 3 or 6 (depending on the size of them and the shot).

Beer Drinking Games

My favorite. Beers drinking games are a part of our journey into manhood. Learn this early and learn this well—join in and have fun, but do not, and I repeat, do not become a champion beer bonger or a champion can shooter and the like.

Your drunken friends cannot remember their names the next day, but they will sure as hell remember that you did the bomb in four seconds, didn't puke, and then asked for more, and guess who will be up at every party until you are well into your sixties.

Group Beer Drinking Games

Again my favorite, but only when I know what the fuck I'm doing. There are too many table games to name, but if you are going to sit at a table with a bunch of people and there are shot glasses waiting to get filled up at the slightest indiscretion, then learn the game before you sit down.

I was considered a wily old veteran until I sat down with some of our finest collegians and played a game involving numbers, pointing, and strange words. Needless to say, forty-five minutes later, I was puking my guts out and seeing little green men. If not, quick on your feet then play beer pong fun, and if you really suck, at least it will only be for twenty-one points and four to six beers. Unless you are stupid enough to challenge that little Chinese bastard again, slip away and move on.

Your Frame of Mind

This is key because it will invariably end up in either a really great night—"Man, is he the funniest guy to hang out with?"—or a bad night—"What an a-hole, fuck it, let's ditch him."

When you head out on the town, don't do so after a big barney with the missus, your girl, or a buddy because you will just ooze a "fuck you" attitude to whoever you are with and wherever you go and you will no doubt bump into another like soul who has a similar "fuck you" attitude. And then guess what.

If you are going to go out with the intent to have a good time, prep yourself. Take a big ass chill pill with the buds before you go out. Meet at someone's house and have a relaxed cold beer or two.

Don't set rigid plans because I guarantee someone will fuck them up by being late, and we all have friends like that—send me

$10 please. Decide on a rough game plan and go with the flow—if five friends say I want to go to this redneck bar and you like rock, get over it and go redneck for one night. It won't kill you.

Next time, you can gently point out, "We went redneck last time and that was, without a doubt, the fattest ugliest chick I have ever done in my life. Tonight we go rock."

Do not go out in threes—yes, that old saying is spot on. Someone will hook up or want to go walk about in search of better pickings, and it will always happen while you are sitting at the bar with the future ex-love of your life or getting ready to swoop in. Go in twos, fours, or more so you always have a wingman—see next chapter for the dos and don'ts on wingmen.

Where You Go

I am not a big believer that a cowboy can't go to a rocker bar any less than a surf dude can't go to a biker bar. See the earlier point—if you go into a biker bar in shorts and flip-flops oozing a "fuck you" attitude, they will be glad to oblige. If you go in with a friendly demeanor, no bad vibes, and show a little respect, you will fit in just fine.

Now, they will give you a ration of shit for looking like a "fag," but get over it, smile, and do *not* respond that they all look like they just got out of jail with very loose buttholes. I did that and barely got away with it.

A final little tip on that front—when you go to the bar or sit down somewhere, say hello to the person next to you; just a little "G'day, how are you doing" will go a long way to setting a tone of civility, and you never know they may strike up a conversation. Some of our best friends have been met in this fashion. "Hey, how are you doing? Good? Rams fan, huh? Yeah, we hate the Raiders, so do we . . . Buffet fans as well. He is coming in a few weeks. Want to go?" And fifteen years later, we are still friends and still hate the Raiders.

Oh, what about bouncers?

(Editors side note: Am I really an editor or a writer? Hell, I don't know, but anyway, you see how this book is evolving. I am sitting here typing, and all of a sudden, I get a big brain fart and realize I missed something—so what about bouncers?)

> Rule number 1: Make friends with them.
> Rule number 2: Make friends with them.

I have spent more than a few hours "bouncing" and for the most part, it is a pretty easy job. Primarily because the A-hole you are chucking out is hammered and you have three or more beefy fuckers to help you.

Now, that isn't always the norm. Occasionally there is a wannabe badass out there who thinks nothing about taking on the bouncers at their own game.

One, of many, incidents comes to mind where I decided to climb a tree in the nightclub that I was in—yes, there was a tree in the middle of the fucking dance floor—guess it was cool back in the '50s—well, I wanted to (a) climb and (b) pee—which I did.

After numerous attempts to dislodge me, which was met with yellow rain and boots, they gave up, turned the lights off, the music back on, and waited for me to get bored. The second I did, they met me with "overwhelming force." After a good kicking, I was actually thrown thru the front door—actually through it. Well, most smart people, as in not drunk and ornery, would lick their wounds and go home. Not smart old me. I went and sat on the beach, had a swig of some cheap wine with a homeless guy, and decided to wait for the bouncers to come out.

What happened next certainly puts a smile on my face, but due to not knowing what the statute of limitations is on assault and the fact that if called out, I won't have to deny anything to stay out of jail, I will move on.

Anyway, back to the beginning on bouncers—wow, what a tangent—make friends with the big ugly, tattooed, broken-nosed, huge-bicep types with zero smiles on their faces. Do not cop an attitude. Heck, even buy them a drink if they are allowed because if and when someone gets in your face and it comes down to them and you, the bouncers might just remember that you were cool before that a-hole started fucking with you—play the game.

Finally, on them—off site they are not bouncers, so if one of them does get out of his realm after crossing the proverbial line between reason and bouncing, as in he/they beat you senseless for no reason when all you did was puke in the bar, find him and kick his teeth in, but remember where he works and never go back there—not like that has ever happened to me, but you get my point. A nod is as good as a wink to a blind bat.

Drunk Driving

You will get caught—yes, you will—look a-hole—yes, you will, the only thing is, where in the trouble range will *you* be when you do Murder or wet reckless?

Getting a DUI is a bitch, no matter when and how you get it. But, and listen up good, you fall asleep in the car, they nab you and you get done. DUI, deal with it, you did the crime, do the time, and in most cases, it will be a bunch of depressing as shit AA meetings and some other classes. Now the other end of the range is that you hit someone and, heaven forbid, kill someone, which is *murder.*

Yes, "murder," and you will go to jail for the rest of your life or for as long as it takes for you to get your butthole stretched by bubba or you turn into the meanest SOB in the big house. Either way, your life is effectively over, and you are fucked in every sense of the word.

Now, taking into account and agreeing that if you do it you will eventually get caught, let's do some planning.

If I said to you, "Give me $50 or $6,000," I have no doubt you will pick the $50. That is likely to be the conservative difference between a taxi and legal fees, fines and classes or anti-drinking machines. Also, I know that when you are happy, happy, joy, joy after twenty beers and ten shots and you have what you "think" is a hot chick on your arm, the last thing on your mind is to catch a cab, especially when you want to show your hottie what you think is your hottie car. All that is going to happen is that you will get your ass arrested, she will have to find a way home, and she will be pissed at the guy (you) who was prepared to jump on a grenade and do her.

And you will wake up trying to decide who is going to give you the least amount of shit to get your cold, drunk, sore ass out of jail.

So once again, agreeing that you will get caught and the fact that your little brain (yes, stupid, the one in your dick) is more powerful on drink than the big one (only slightly), there are some things you can do.

1. Get to where you are going, dump off everyone, find a safe parking area, and find a way to lock your keys in the car. Either lock the doors before you close them, crack a window low enough to slide the keys in but not low enough for you and your drunk buddies who have somehow found a coat hangar at three in the morning to pull them out.

   Or give them to a bartender, which is not ideal because you can put enough pressure on them to give them back to you. If you do this on a regular basis, you will find it gets to be a habit and not a big deal.

2. Designate a driver. Personally not my favorite, unless it is someone other than me. Being a designated driver is a bitch when everything that their drunk friends think as being "fucking hilarious" generally isn't to the poor slob who is driving them around, trying to find breakfast, a titty bar, a liquor store, or a place to shag without getting caught.

So unless you command the respect that comes with a statement such as "Hey, dickheads, I am the designated driver tonight, and while I will take you out and about and home, I will not tolerate anyone puking in my car, directions from anyone, farting above six decibels, and bean burritos before I drop your asses off. And no ugly chicks in my car. If you want to take that horror home, get a cab," don't be the DD.

3. Get your cheap ass buddies to pony up before they go out for a to-and-from cab fare. Meet at a central house and party down. See earlier suggestion, catch a cab to the first bar in a good area and do your thing.

    Have enough in the kitty to catch a round trip to people's home and then get them their keys the next day. Now, don't trust anyone with the kitty, like me FOR EXAMPLE, I will take that taxi kitty and will go walk about, find food, a titty bar and a late-night drinking spot, a clean bush (one with leaves), and then sometime when the sun comes up, catch a cab to get me home while my former mates are cussing me out.

4. Don't take responsibility for anyone. Just do not take your car, make sure you wear a seat belt, and if they are too drunk to drive and they refuse to give you the keys, then take charge and catch your own cab home. Hopefully they will get a lower scale of DUI pain than the top painful and life changing one.

    Don't drink and drive, because unlike most of the other nightmares that I list in this book, you will find it hard to recover. Fat chicks sometimes get skinny, and you can hide for six months if you have to. Black eyes and thick lips from getting your ass kicked will heal. Arrested for being drunk in public, a misdemeanor, so who gives a shit? Big fucking deal. But a DUI—the Horror, as in Apocalypse Now!

Meetings with a bunch of so-called ex-alchie losers, equipment in the car, which is very embarrassing when taking your mum to lunch. NO second chances. You will go to jail, and now they even have ankle bracelets to detect alcohol—Jesus, that would suck.

Finally there is a reason why this (drinking) is the first chapter, and it is this.

Simply put, very few of us need the advice in the following chapters if we do not drink. We do not generally get in fights, jump off bridges, fuck fat chicks, and on and on. So as you read on, open another beer and take into account that most of the shit we *will* get into *will* revolve around drinking—trust me.

CHAPTER 2

FIGHTING

fight

Function: *verb*

Date: before 12th century

1: to contend in battle or physical combat; *especially* **:** to strive to overcome a person by blows or weapons
2: to engage in boxing (yeah right)

Fighting is an interesting part of life. Some of us will never have a "quote on quote" punch-up, and some of us will have many. Fighting seems to revolve around many factors, which I will help you recognize. The key ones are your environment, the opposition, and what are you prepared to do.

Environment is key because that should tell you what kind of response you should get when you are in "transmit" instead of "receive" mode. Transmitting is when you are flapping your gums instead of receiving the message; receiving is when you listen and realize that what is being said could come true and if it does, it will be painful.

You can give or receive the message, that is up to you, but the message is simple—you are about to kick someone's ass, or you are about to get yours handed to you.

If you are going to go into a biker bar in a three-piece suit, a Raider bar wearing a Charger shirt or a bar where you are definitely in the minority, then you better receive and not transmit. However, on the other side of the scale, if you go into a bar full of your favorite yuppies, you can probably transmit like a space probe and end up with nothing more than an "American Bar Fight."

"What's an American bar fight?" you might say. Well, don't get me wrong, but that is the yuppie version of a real fight. It starts with a few beers and maybe a few shots and you decide that you do not like someone or, heaven forbid, someone bumped into you. "Hey, man, what is your problem?" is generally the first shot in the barrage. What generally happens is that voices get raised, chests get bigger, friends get involved, and . . . *no and*.

The raised voices have drawn the attention of the bar staff and bouncers. Now I'm not saying the contestants are looking for the large help to arrive, but they will verbalize, "I am going to kick your ass," and maybe point a finger or two, etc., right up to the point when the bouncers get there; then, they will finally decide to throw a punch.

Of course, by this time, no one is going to get hurt. Everyone can walk away, saying, "I would have kicked his ass," and you still have all the buttons on your shirt. Actually, not a bad scenario when it comes down to it as opposed to the real world.

In the real world, and yes, there is one out there. You better look the hell out and make some very conscious decisions on whether the road you are about to take is worth it. If you are thinking of going, then go—don't fuck around, go.

Are you going to brake or push the accelerator? Are you going to stand or fall? Run or walk? Heck, I am running out of analogies, but your chances of survival are better if you punch hard and, most importantly, *first*.

Next comes the opposition. This is the hard part. There are so many different equations that you have to be careful. I personally laid out a huge muscle bound bouncer with just two punches. I have also seen a very small man beat the living crap out of a nasty big biker type. Just because someone has tats, scars, or a Mohawk, it doesn't automatically make him a bad ass, and do not assume that the quiet, unassuming guy in the shirt and tie is a wimp.

So rule one is avoid fights, rule two is recognize who you are fighting, and rule three is don't make assumptions because some of that kung fu movie shit *is* spot on.

I spend a little time, when I go into a bar, checking the people out. You can tell who is who for the most part. Look for broken noses and cauliflower ears. Why? Because the pussies of the world who got a broken nose got it fixed—real fighters don't. Cauliflower ears are a sign of constant pressure and grinding on what is, traditionally, a floppy soft piece of flesh. If it looks like a knot of rubber, be nice. Sports like boxing, wrestling, martial arts, rugby all come to mind when I see a cauliflower ear or two. As to body type, I look first at forearms, "Why, man, I have been doing curls to build my 'ceps for years now?"

Simply put, gripping strength is the core to grappling strength and then onto punching strength. If someone has thirty-six-inch biceps and three-inch forearms, feel free to kick his ass. If the person you notice has cord iron forearms with the appropriate amount of veins, then package that with nice-sized biceps, broken nose, and cauliflower ears, then beware.

Those people are, for the most part, super nice because they don't have anything to prove. But rest assured, rub them the wrong way and they will readjust your sinuses and your testicles all in one go.

So assuming that you completely ignored the previous paragraph, my simple rule of thumb is that if you are sure that it is going to come to blows, hit hard, hit fast, and don't stop until he is on the floor and not looking to get back up. Of course, if you do not want to go to jail on a regular basis (once in a while is not that bad of a life lesson—see the law chapter), be careful on how and when you make that decision.

This is my gauge on whether it is time to go or not.

Try to picture this, and it is always hard to picture anything written in a book. Imagine that your face is a speedometer with two speeds: 0-50 = *stop* and 50-100 = *go*.

If the needle is in the *stop* area, then this is your time to really show off and be cocky. You have made the decision that the person, or persons, you are arguing with are not really a threat to your general well-being.

You can be a smart ass, make him look bad in front of his girlfriend or buddies, be nice and offer to buy him a drink, and generally talk your way out of the situation all without breaking a sweat.

If the needle hits fifty-one or is in the *go* area, then shut the fuck up and connect your forehead rapidly with the bridge of their nose. Followed promptly with a kick in the balls, a right cross, and, if he still hasn't hit the deck, a knee to the face while holding the back of his head with both hands.

That should be the end of story, if not, you are in deep shit. ☺ Now rapidly back up and leave the area as quickly as possible and *do not go back there* for at least a month or so because he will be back with his buddies looking to even the score.

Now as to what you are prepared to do, many of you will not find that out until it is too late; and when you do, it might be a shock. My weapon of choice used to be the forehead. So if you are an American and the person you are fucking with is European, look out. If you think, "Why is he getting closer and starting to look like he is going to kiss me?"

He is. It means he is lining up to give you the good old-fashioned Scottish kiss that will end up with any of the following: busted nose—you can't see what's coming next; ringing head, where he missed your nose—you still can't see what's coming next; teeth flying across the room—where you don't give a fuck what's coming next because it's too late because whatever else happens, it won't be as painful as your jaw the next morning.

So taking into account that you may be a novice at the fine art of bar fighting, consider these tips—and this one is even more huge than the big *but* (not *butt*, you pervert) I mentioned earlier. Be careful what you try and practice; maybe on that rubber doll hidden under your bed.

A good option is the good old-fashioned "eight-ouncer"—a punch, not a steak, you idiot—to the nose: generally good, pretty easy to execute, and generally gets good results, especially if the fight is broken up before the fucker gets back up.

There is the head butt, which I have covered; however, you will look like a major tosser if you miss and you will receive the next shot.

Kick in the balls—another favorite of mine. Do not aim for their balls with your toes, aim with your shins. They will be able to jump back a few inches so you should catch them just right. If not, you will miss and again look stupid and get a wallop or two before you recover. The good thing about a successful kick in the balls is that they will invariably grab their nuts with *both* hands, leaving themselves open for all sorts of follow-up.

So taking into account that you are now educated on the martial art of bar fighting, sorry; but on that note, if you do take martial arts, they are the best form of self-defense going. However, the discipline and control involved only kicks in around a brown belt. So if you have been doing Karate for a few months and have just gotten your yellow belt, don't take on that Randy Couture—looking motherfucker by attempting a round house kick to his noggin'—*you will die.*

For the record, those know-it-alls who say it is harder to walk away from a confrontation than it is to fight are full of shit or grew up in a prep school for girls, have never been drunk in a bar, or are black belts in the martial arts and know they could kill the stupid motherfucker messing with them, with their thumbs.

For the rest of us, walking away can lead to more BS than it may be worth, so think twice if you encounter the following:

1. The person you are arguing with calls you a pussy and refuses to let you walk away—in fact, he keeps pushing you in the chest or the back until he gets a physical reaction. By this time, the needle is way into the *go* area. Remember the fifty-one plus rule, kick his ass with every ounce of strength you have and make sure that when you have finished, he knows you didn't want any trouble in the first place.

2. You back down and your mates call you a puss for the rest of your life. The options here are limited but effective. Challenge any and all of your friends to a one-on-one if they do not drop it. If they are real friends, they will say "Nah, that's alright," and move on—if they are not real friends, you can prove to be "unpusslike" by kicking your future ex-friends' asses effectively making the "puss" label disappear forever.

Some people are complete dickheads and deserve a butt kicking—I didn't get my first one until I was forty plus years old, and then it was a good wake-up call.

CHAPTER 3

FUCKING

fuck·ing

Function: *adjective or adverb*

Date: 1893 (*not according to the movies*)

1. Man's version of the female words "to make love"
2. Descriptive of the state someone is in e.g.—a train is heading toward their car, which is stalled on the tracks—they are fucked
3. Flying down a mountain and a ski falls of—you are fucked
4. Bad ass dude decides to kick your ass—you are fucked
5. You just ran from the cops and they caught you—you are fucked
6. You got caught cheating on an exam—you are fucked
7. The boys saw that skanky ho you were with last night—you are fucked

You get the point, *Webster* didn't have a good definition for me to use (I wonder why) so I made up my own. ☺

Yeah, baby, this should be fun. Why? Because I think, like the rest of you, that I am very good at it or used to be in my younger pre-Viagra days. ☺

That being said, let's be clear, it is not *fucking*, it is making love (me pandering to the women), but for reasons of clarity, I am going to refer to it as *fucking*.

Note: I am not sure what the Guinness book of records is for using the word *fuck* or *fucking* in one chapter, but there is a good chance that I will own it once we are finished with this diatribe.

So I am thinking once again while I am writing/typing, *How the hell do I map this out?* I could, say, put together top ten rules, use some examples (but that might get me in trouble), chitchat about it, or a combo of all three—yep, that's the way to go.

TOP TEN THINGS TO REMEMBER WHEN FUCKING

1. Do it with a woman, or two—sorry, but I am a homophobe; and if that costs me in the world of political correctness, then fuck off—don't read any further and ask for a refund.
2. Size does not matter, as in the size of your dick, the size of her vagina, or the size of her in general. Many of you will look at some big porker and go, "Oh my god, someone jump on that grenade." Wrong—she could be the best fuck you have ever had or have even dreamed about. On the other side, that babe that you have been chasing for weeks, who has cost you a small fortune in dinner and drinks and who has big tits, blonde hair, and a nice peachy little ass, could, when you finally get to nail her (oops, missed an opportunity to use fuck)—when you finally fuck her—it could be like fucking a two-week-old cod. As to the good old-fashioned penis, dick, prick, terminator, one-eyed trouser python, Eisenhower in my case, etc., size is not the issue—it is how you move and shake it. My good friend John (real name) has a great saying,

which I will plagiarize without his permission—fuck him, he owes me.

"Hi, my name is John. I don't have a big dick. The one I have is two inches long and three inches round, *but* look the fuck out because I've got 260 pounds pushing it in." Personally, on the dick front once again, I think mine is perfect of course. Not too long, as in it doesn't get in the way when not in use. Not too thick, don't want to stretch the poor girl out.

It has a slight right-hand curve, which is good for hunting down that elusive G-spot (if there is such a thing)—I know there is one but since women keep moving the fucker around it is better to treat it like the Holy Grail and just keep trying to find it. When you do look out it could start raining down there. And all in all, it functions pretty good except for an annoying foreskin. See chitchat for some fun on that subject. Jesus H—this is like a whole chapter on size. Now to our selected chickadee—size does matter to them, selfish bastards. You just have to overcome their needs and desires with sneakiness and stamina and the occasional commando tactic.

3. Women's pussies can be like a rosebud on a balmy sunny day or like a three-week-old fish taco. Beauty is in the eye of the beholder when it comes to a women's pussy, glut box, receptacle, etc. The key here is just like when you are scoping out the bar and you see the porker and think, *No way*, pussies can be just like that. Oooo, fuck, that looks nasty, but inside they have muscles that will milk you like a cow and leave you a jellied mess on the floor. There is this thing hidden somewhere between "John Wayne's saddle bags," my favorite euphemism for piss flaps, called a *clit*.

This little bastard is the key to the world of fucking just like the G Spot. Shit, I wish I had this book and someone as good as me to tell me about it a lot earlier. That elusive little fucker can save you a lot of embarrassment. Now, I am not talking about me—but, say, *you* are the type of guy that pretty much sticks it in, wiggles it around, and then zoweee, over and out. Spending a little time on the little bastard will get her a little closer to her happy place than she would be if you routinely come in thirty seconds.

4. Hairiness (when chitchatting about pussies) is also key—they range from completely shaved (California) to a thicket, a big bush—dumbass, of nasty unfriendly rough hair (French), so the middle ground is good; nice little trimmed runway (without lights) to guide you on your way. Shaved completely, nightmare, unless you get there the minute after the event; if you don't know what I am talking about, get your dick out and rub it against some sandpaper for, say, ten minutes or maybe lick some sandpaper for ten minutes—either way, you should get my point. The big bush—yuck!—Jesus Christ, women, trim that fucker down. Think about us for a minute and also think about your own hygiene.

   By the time we have riffled through the hair to get to where we are heading and where we assume you women want us to go, we have hair up our noses, in our teeth, and it is not nice having to spit midway in. And to cap it off, we have a much lessened chance to say hello to *our little friend* (name that movie) for all the camouflage it is hidden in. Finally, when juices start to flow down there from both directions, it can get pretty nasty real quick, so *trim it—now!*

5. FIND A SQUIRTER . . . See now I've done it. Many men will go thru life wondering what the hell a squirter is. Well simply put it is that rare woman who comes with so much conviction that fluid of some kind, no sorry I have no idea what it is and since I cannot Google "Female Vagina Squirt Juice" without getting sent to thousands of porn sites . . . Hold . . . Hold . . . No, back to it is fluid of some kind. My first entry into the

squirt realm was some lovely lady sitting on my face and telling me that she loves me when all of sudden I am drowning. At first I thought she pissed on me, nasty bitch, until I realized she was a soggy mess, not just down below but from head to toe with orgasm aftershocks. Once I realized what the fuck was going on there was no stopping me—go find a squirter before it is too late.

6. Now let's transition from fucking to making love. Yup, there is a difference. Fucking is more of a pagan ritual that takes mutual consent and a lot of grunting. Some women like fucking; some like making love. You are a genius if you can really work out the difference, but let me give you some thoughts to consider on the difference.

First off, it shouldn't take you long to work out if the girl you are with prefers fucking or making love. Turn her over, mount her like you mean it, grab her hair, and hang on for the ride. If you find yourself flying through the air and her sitting with her back to the headboard, she likes making love.

Oh, and don't go the anal sex route until at least testing the water (well, you know) with your finger—try putting the python in there without permission and say bye-bye. So assuming that she likes to "make love," stay away from that particular brown eye.

Consideration number 1—your stamina, as in, do you come the second she takes her clothes off or does it take you three days with breaks in between. If the former, do all you can to get her off before you go to happyville.

The easiest way is to keep her grubby little hands of your tadger until you are good and ready. Gently does it there, big boy—play, lick, cuddle, nibble, use everything else but Eisenhower. When you feel she is close, invade and conquer. Once you get that timing down pat, you can work on your own longevity; remember, she comes first, you are a stud; you come first and she is looking over your shoulder. Also remember that once you come, Eisenhower is going to sleep, and all the wiggling and movement in the world isn't going to hit that all-elusive G-spot, unless of course you are on Viagra, which at your age is not good.

Consideration number 2 is how nasty is she? All women have a range from *frigid* to the *infernos of hell*. Someone in the middle is generally best for your overall health and well-being. With women, you can never judge a book by its cover. They can wear full-length dresses, baggy sweaters, and when in the sack, fuck you so you cannot walk for a week—on the other hand, that slutty-looking bitch with the fake boobs, short skirt, and pouty lips can leave you wanting and wondering was it worth the chase. No rhyme or reason, just the way it is, and you can only hope that one day you find that ying to your yang as the perfect bedmate.

7. *Post-Fucking decorum*—this is always fun. From snoring and falling asleep midstride to getting up and making breakfast. My opinion on this is it depends upon where the girl in question fits in your importance category. "One-night stand" or "wow, is she the one?" If a one-night stand, slowly open one eye while making sure not to wake her and check her out. Lift the covers, see is if she is a porker or a nymph, check her face out, nice looking with limited make up or with a face looking like the surface of Mars. Try to clear your head. Was she a good fuck, lousy, nasty, or boring?

So if fat, ugly, and a lousy fuck, get out of there quick and clean and don't go back to that bar *ever* again. If by chance she is lying on your arm, do the "double coyote" (mentioned earlier). Now, that is worse-case scenario. What about a bit of a porker, pretty face, and fucks like a rabbit. Well, she might not be in line for a major date with the boys, but you might want to line her up for a regular bootie call.

Okay, you dipshit—"bootie call"—when you go out drinking with the boys, you strike out with the lookers, get drunk, strike out with the ugly ones, get drunker, but you can always swing by "Susie's" for cuddles, as in drunk sex.

Bootie calls are something that every man should have lined up at least once in their miserable lives.

Don't underestimate the chickadee. You are a bootie call to her as well, and the second you fall down on the job, she will find a suitable stand-in.

Also, the second she tries to transition from bootie call to "let's go on a date"—do the pros and cons list and make a decision that you don't mind seeing her more or educate her to where she fits in the whole scheme of things and let her decide. Either way, don't be an a-hole. Deal with it and move on, and don't fuck it up for her next boyfriend/bootie call by calling every time you are out on the town fucked up at three in the morning.

Last but not the least option, "Holy shit, this girl is amazing, funny, sensual with an underlying I-am-going-to-fuck-your-brains-out feel," nice figure, no makeup, clean hair, trimmed down below (thought I was going to forget that, didn't ya?), and someone who you wouldn't mind the boys seeing you with. Now at the first chance you have, clean your teeth—no one is going to want a dawn strike that begins by kissing the inside of Grandpa's bedroom slipper. Then pee and crimp your foreskin and flush it out, or if no flapper, wash your willy in the sink. You do not want this woman to think about giving you a blow job for breakfast only to find last night's cheese hanging around.

Okay, assuming you are nice and clean now, *do not* just jump back into bed and try to roger (fuck) the shit out of her again. Once you have taken care of the hygiene, snuggle up and see what she does. If she snuggles back, you did a fair to middling job last night; if she gets up and leaves the bedroom, one of two things is going on.

One, she is ashamed that she had sex with you, or two, you sucked and she doesn't want to have sex with you again.

Either way, be cool until you know which is which. If she snuggles, snuggle back; if she reaches for Eisenhower, give it to her good. If she just snuggles (god, how gay am I for using that word so much), give it a few minutes and get up and make her some breakfast. If you don't know how to make a semi-decent breakfast, go home to Mum's for the weekend and learn the fuck how. If you can make breakfast and can chat without it being awkward, as in you get the feeling that she is wondering what the hell just happened, hang for a while.

If more sex presents itself, great; if not, politely get out of there with a promise to call. *Do not* try to be too studly by not calling. If you like this girl, call later that day and thank her for a great time. *No*, that does not mean leave a voice mail saying, "Wow, that was awesome. You can fuck like a rabbit. Can we do it again?" Reach her live. If not, leave a message asking if you can take her out to dinner or something. I know, I know, it is really tempting to leave the other message. ☺

8. Did I say ten comments? Holy crap, that is going to be a push. Protection seems to come to mind. This will be short—if you are going to fuck someone you don't know, wear a condom. Not much thinking there, is there? Personally, I hate the fucking things, but there are reasons they sell millions of them and they are in fancy colors, ribbed, tasty (fuck you, no, I haven't tried one), and of different sizes. Look at it this way, don't wear one, what can happen? Hmm, first off, she can get pregnant, nightmare of nightmares. If she is a non-Catholic or should I say non-practicing, you can cough up the fee to terminate it—okay, abortion—hate that word. If she doesn't want to go down that road, your life is over as you know it.

Don't believe it for one second when she says, "It's okay, I will raise it (it's actually not a baby in her mind yet) on my own." Bull-fucking-shit—the second mini you is born, you are on the hook, support payments, babysitting, shoulder to cry on, dealing with her loser boyfriends who hate the fact she has a kid, and thousands of other less-than-pleasurable situations. Also don't believe for one second when you say, "It's okay, I'll do the right thing and stick by you." Bull-fucking-shit. You may think that until you realize that the chick you knocked up is a total loser and you can't stand to be around the bitch. Kind of hard to be supportive when it is a fine line between wanting to kill her or yourself.

Oh, and by the way, good luck finding anyone else to marry either of you. She has no chance. Who the hell wants to start a family with a single mum who got knocked up by some loser who didn't feel the need to marry her in the first place? For you, good luck dropping that bombshell. "Oh, honey, by the way, I have a son/daughter with some slut who fucked me one night and we didn't use a condom." If you expect, "That's okay, I understand," you are out of your fucking mind. Hmmm, why else would you wear a condom?

Okay, pretend I am actually asking a question and now you answer it for me—mentally, think of the theme to *Jeopardy*: der, der, derrrr, de der de derrr . . . Okay, what is the answer? Yes, stupid, because you will catch something nasty, "No, I won't." "Yes, you will."

I remember a good friend of mine (sorry "ED"); one night, we were out dressed to the nines when this vision walked into the club. White chiffon dress, legs up to her ears, tits to die for, blonde, and beautiful. She walked up to buddy boy and asked him to dance—he nearly shit. Five hours later, he is fucking the shit out of her in her apartment. Five days later, he is getting a penicillin shot in his ass—which really hurts—or so I've heard. Again, no rhyme or reason, skanky-looking ho might be cleaner because nobody but drunks like you will fuck her. However, slutty babe who just likes dick will have every disease under the sun. Take the danger out of the mix.

Wear a condom and fuck everything you can without a care in the world. Is that not sage advice? Damn, that was longer than expected.

9. Ooh, good, just managed to think of another one. Sex and marriage. Simple: when you get married, your sex life will decrease; when you have kids, it will decrease even more; and when you hit fifty, forget it. Okay, that is too simple, and it wouldn't be a very long book if I quit there, so . . .

Fucking, to a lot of women, is not as important as it is to a lot of men. What is important to them is the other pieces of the proverbial pie—partner, family, home, and everything that goes along with it, and so it should be to you as well. No matter what, men still want to fuck. The problem is that once you get married, the fucking had better be with the same person, yes, the missus, er, indoors, she who must be obeyed or the one with tits who wears the pants.

The way to look at it is like this. Imagine that proverbial pie as a real one—a big fat juicy apple pie—yummy, yummy. Well, you sit down and begin to chow, and after eating nine pieces, you find that the last piece isn't tasting just right, and you feel a little sick. The problem is you ate too much and didn't know when to stop. Life is like that, and so is marriage.

This is how your "life pie" might look if neatly sliced up.

1st slice—great wife
2nd slice—she is also your best friend
3rd slice—you have kids who are healthy and happy
4th slice—you live in a nice home
5th slice—you have enough financial security to pay the bills
6th slice—you have a small group of good friends
7th slice—you have a nice car
8th slice—a big screen TV
9th slice—and there is always beer in the fridge

And your world comes crashing down because number 10 is as follows:

10th slice—you don't get laid anymore, a blow job is a distant memory, and drunk sex just never happens because it is too easy to pass out and feign unconsciousness.

That's it, life is over—*not!* Take the good pieces of the pie and be grateful. Don't fuck up your life by making number 10 more important than the other nine.

If you do decide to, once again, ignore my sage advice and you cannot keep your dick in your pants, then be smart about it. I am not going to be holier than though and act like it doesn't happen, but if your balls are that full, you have plenty of options. Just take this advice and don't "have an affair." If you are stupid enough to have an affair, then come to terms with the fact that you will get caught and life as you know it is over. You have fucked some bitch who doesn't give a shit about you or your family, you have fucked your wife, figuratively; as in, she will never trust you again. You have fucked your kids because they will never understand why you don't live at home anymore. You have fucked your friends because they will not want to be caught in the middle of a divorce. You have fucked your bill-paying capability paying child support. You may keep the car and the big screen, but not likely, and your little beer fridge in the studio apartment you live in will make you want to weep.

So in short, you have an affair and you have effectively taken a royal-sized shit in your "life pie," and it will be inedible forevermore. If you want to get your nut off, do it somewhere else. Out of town, don't shit on your own doorstep.

Go to a "massage" parlor and get a rub and a tug with a happy ending. Bash it yourself, and if that doesn't work, sit on your hand for an hour before you do to make it numb so you don't know who is doing it. But to be clear, do *not* have an affair, as in going on dates, getting hotel rooms with her, going on vacation, being seen out and about. Don't give her your name, and sure as fuck, don't let her know where you live.

Do not lie to her and say that you aren't married because when she finds out, she will be the psycho bitch from hell who will think nothing of turning up on your doorstep for a chat and a cup of tea with the missus.

Okay, enough said on that one—fuck, how many comments left? Oh, just one, kind of like being "just" five hundred yards from the summit of Everest; I know that's a little dramatic, just getting serious with you as to how fucking hard it really is to write this book—*not*—see, I was fucking kidding all the way.

Okay—one to go, more *Jeopardy* music. Okay, got one; no, I don't. More music, okay, what about?

Nope, oh fuck it—I will send this chapter to a mate who will give me some suggestions, I am sure. If not, nine out of ten ain't half bad.

PS on this chapter and to save you the trouble because I know you're going to go back and count how many times I say *fuck* in this chapter (yes, you are), the total is fifty-one. But since I had fifty-five in mind, I just want to say I cannot fucking believe that you are still reading this fucking book and how have you not been fucking offended by the content, especially the use of the *fuck* word and its derivatives. In short, you are one sick fuck who should go get some fucking help. Oh crap, that is fifty-eight now. Fuck it, I might as well go for sixty fucks in one fucking chapter—now it is sixty-one—damn, enough for fuck's sake, damn sixty-two, you are losing your fucking mind—sixty-three. ☺

CHAPTER 4

GAMBLING

gam·ble

Function: *verb*

Date: 1772

1a: to play a game for money or property **b:** to bet on an uncertain
outcome
2: to stake something on a contingency: take a chance

This will be short and sweet, as will most of the rest of this
book, so let me start by saying don't do it. Now, taking into
account that you are going to gamble in some way, shape, or form,
let's try to see if we can do it a little better and a little smarter
than I have.

If you gamble on a regular basis, you will end up losing, pure
and simple, but how much and the impact that it will have is up
to you. Gambling is very much like drinking; it can be addictive,
and it, very rarely, has a good consequence.

The range of gambling is from betting the missus on who gets kicked off the reality show of choice to manic gambling where every simple event is a bet.

Lakers to win by four with a total of over 190 points for the game. With ninety in the first and eighty in the second half, and Kobe will score more than thirty-two points and not less than twenty. His balls will fall out of his shorts at exactly three minutes twenty seconds into the second period. Jack will fart at exactly six minutes and twenty-two seconds into the third period. They will show at least one big pair of knockers at least five times during the game and focus on at least one celebrity during the game. You get my drift?

I am lucky—I know very little about American sports (or any other for that matter). So I am reluctant to bet on sports, but it makes me very dangerous when betting with me on things like trivia, history, geography, and the like.

My game of choice is poker, and there is more than one reason. The analogy that I use is this: You can have fun at poker and lose. You can have fun at poker and win. But you can also win and "not" have fun. The final one sucks, losing and not having fun.

Sitting around with some friends, drinking beers, smoking cigars, telling nasty stories about women you knew, and playing a game of chance is fun; if you win, all the better.

The key part of gambling is quitting while you are ahead. Don't believe for one minute that it is easy to do—it's not. If you can stay sober enough to quit while up the odds are with you. If you insist on playing indefinitely, you will end up losing it all, and some. Alternatively, have some good friends who are big enough to manhandle you to your room or take the money off you.

My best session ever was in Australia—drunk like a Black Santa Claus on the 4th of July and I decide to go to the Casino. I warm up by playing Black Jack and driving everyone insane not just because of the way I was playing but because I was winning.

By mid afternoon I am five grand up and have no friends left because I kept splitting tens, kings and I refused to take a card when the book says I should.

Feeling no pain I went downstairs to play Pai Gow—never played it before but after about 2 hours I became an instant celebrity.

When I sat down I was the only person at the table by the time I finished I had 40 little Asian fuckers wondering how the hell I was winning. It did not help that my large friend from Chicago was shouting out "he crazy round eyes" every time I won. Twelve Thousand Dollars "UP" and my renewed friends finally manhandled me to bed.

Funny as shit first thing in the morning when the boys stream into my room and throw thousands of dollars into the air—nothing with get rid of a bitch of a hangover quicker than being showered by money, money and more money.

Now the moral of this story is the end result. We get up start drinking again, put on our suits and ties on and off we go to The Melbourne Cup the biggest horse race in the world and at the same time the biggest drunk fest. To sum it best I must quote the taxi driver and please think Aussie accent "first time here mate? Well you will love it. Thousands of women come here dressed like princesses and four hours later they leave looking like whores".

My god how true he was.

I should have known I was in trouble when we went to the VIP tent and they asked what I would like—I casually replied "champagne" to which they replied "how many glasses" to which I replied—straight faced—"none just give me three bottles of Dom".

Leaving Melbourne 36 hours later I was back to square one—no winnings just a wonderful memory.

So the moral of the story is if you do wake up in the morning with a wad of cash, put it in the mail or your bank account and go have some fun with a small portion of it. Do not go back to the casino and gamble again—the best of the best don't win two days in a row.

The bottom line it is *all* luck—if you think you are a good craps player you are full of just that—crap.

Roulette—same thing, it could land on black a thousand times, and there is no guarantee that it will land on black on spin 1,001.

Poker's lots of fun; with your buddies, throw caution to the wind. Casinos play tight and don't bluff. There will always be some drunk a-hole who will call you and luck out with a higher kicker.

Blackjack, boring stupid game with a bunch of a-holes telling you what to do. I say fuck 'em—if you want to split kings, then do it. It's your money, not theirs. My attitude is that if I am not in the game, I cannot win, so fuck them and their take-a-card-on-fourteen bullshit.

Finally, if you are smart, you will play nickel slots—make friends with the cocktail waitress and get absolutely fucked up for as little as ten bucks—then go to the bar and act like a high roller. If you do win in a casino (not likely) and they comp your shit, great; if you lose, then come to terms with the fact that each one of those "free" Heinekens cost you approximately $150 each—justify it any way you like.

CHAPTER 5

CONFIDENCE

con-fi-dence

Function noun:

Date: 1350-1400

1. full trust; belief in the powers, trustworthiness, or reliability of a person or thing: *We have every confidence in their ability to succeed.*
2. Belief in oneself and one's powers or abilities; self-confidence; self-reliance; assurance: *His lack of confidence defeated him.*
3. certitude; assurance: *He described the situation with such confidence that the audience believed him completely.*

A mate of mine who was good enough to review my dribble made a good point. "But you are a confident mother fucker because of who you are and what you have done in life, everyone is not like you" . . .

Good point—shit I really do have some smart friends.

Confidence, later on in this book I talk about be confident, confident and more confident. Confidence can come in many forms and it can manifest itself in many ways. Whether defending your honor or trying to get "On Her" confidence will give the recipient cause to pause in how they deal with you and how you are conducting yourself.

When I was growing up I was the biggest pussy going (until 12 years old) and once I joined the military it didn't take me long to realize that I had better man up to a whole new level or life was going to be miserable.

Week one after joining her Majesty's Armed Forces some blowhard who got nominated to become class leader pegged me as a "trouble maker" and decided in return to nominate me as his whipping boy.

After a couple of days that rapidly came to an end when he said "hey clean that shit up" and I responded with a swift smack to his nose. Of course I peeled potatoes for 5 days straight but you know what a couple of good things happened. I immediately got a reputation as someone who shouldn't be fucked with and the "former" class leader learned some basic leadership skills—you earn respect you don't pin it on your shirt.

Not long after that an example of supreme confidence in the face of certain death, well not death but certainly and major ass whooping. I was walking back to base one night from some chickadees house and a local civilian group/gang blocked my path. After some friendly banter it was obvious that they had every intention—five to one—to kick my ass. Where this confidence came from I don't know since I was barely 17 at the time but it worked.

I moved forward into the group and got up close to the leader where I offered him some sage advice. "Well now, it looks like you lot have every intention to give me a good beating. Well let me tell YOU how it is going to go. You (the leader) are going to get fucked up before they even get a shot on me. You (another likely leader) are going to get some damage and the rest of you might get away unscathed.

But before we begin rest assured that I am going to be in this neighborhood for at least another 6 months and I will find each and every one of you and I *will* give you a good kicking".

Their head honcho thought about it for all of 10 seconds and then decided that we should part ways with a simple comment "you better watch your back you wanker" . . .

The point here is there is no doubt in my mind that my handsome good looks were going deteriorate pretty rapidly once they got going but you know what I had nothing to lose so what the fuck, go for it. Many things in life are like that, just weigh up the pros and cons and decide what have you really got to lose and go for it.

Over the years I challenged myself in many ways and with success I got more and more confident to the point where I felt comfortable in any situation that came my way.

Whether talking to the King or the Janitor, the Princess or the Whore, the boss or my employee. I can adapt and only because I am confident.

So if you are miserable in your job? tell them to fuck off and find something that you enjoy. In a relationship that is not working? then break it off and wait for something better to come along.

I fondly remember being in Gothenburg Sweden having a cold beer and ogling a sizable group of good looking women (sorry side note, Scandinavians are the hottest women in the world by a long shot and I have sampled my fair share of women around the world). Okay. So I am surrounded by great looking women and this goddess walks in and head towards the bar "keep coming, keep coming"—YES. She is right next to me, she turns to me and says "hello" in a come in your pants accent. I reply "holy shit, you are fucking gorgeous" . . . Oh crap. No, oh crap, she replies, "thank you can I buy you a drink" . . .

Four days of heaven later as a guest of her vagina and her parents lake house and life was as it should be—Fucking-A good.

You can gain confidence in many ways—look around you and study people and you will see and feel who are really confident. There is no reason, none, that you cannot be just as confident. You cannot buy confidence but you can learn it.

Find something that you think challenges you. It could range from jumping out of an aircraft when you know it is going to scare you shitless (just like me) or it can be a test or course that you don't think you can do or pass.

It can be get up in front of the class and sing a song, ask the hottest girl out on a date or tell the school bully to fuck off if he picks on you. No matter the end result you will be better for it.

"Damn I cannot believe I jumped out of a perfectly good plane, bet your ass I am going to buy that skydivers do it higher t-shirt".

"Fuck I am the worst singer ever, but man, it gave the whole class a good giggle"

"Holy shit she said yes, now what the fuck am I supposed to do"

AND "Okay, so he kicked my ass but that sympathy fuck from Jane J. was worth it" . . .

Don't confuse confidence with bluster and aggression. If you come across as being full of shit you negate the coolness of being confident and someone will call you on it and then you will look like a horses ass if you cannot deliver.

A good example of quiet confidence is when I was younger and in amazing shape I intentionally used to wear baggy shirts.

Other mates of mine would wear skin tight shirts with the sleeves rolled up to show their gun's. I always felt I didn't need to show off.

I knew I had the tools and knew how to use them so why flaunt them. I found out very early than women like nothing better than to sneak that touchy feely little grip on the arm to see what's hidden under there and when they do it is like "wow, this guy is buffed and he is confident enough to not show it".

Like I said confidence can't be bought but you will be surprised how easy it can be gained.

CHAPTER 6

THE LAW, LAWYERS, THE MAN, ETC.

LAW

Function: Noun

Date: Since the beginning of time

Jesus Fucking Christ—most words have a couple of descriptives but *Law* has twenty-one plus, so sod it back to my definitions again.

1. What some people put in place to get other people to do what they want
2. What people with badges and guns enforce
3. What wimpy motherfuckers use when things don't go their way
4. What lawyers invent so that they can self-perpetuate their lives by suing people and/or defending the laws they invented in the first place
5. Things that have been in place since the beginning of time and will be there until the end. Lawyers are like cockroaches—no matter what happens in the world, they will always survive—hence, the reason why most politicians are lawyers
6. Six thru twenty-one, come up with your descriptives

Love or hate it, or them, we need it and them; nearly choked to death then and there. We all whine about cops and lawyers, and most of the time, it is because we fucked up in some way or form and was on the receiving end of their attention.

Let's look at cops right off the bat—I have met good and bad ones in all kinds of settings. I have met some cops socially who have the personality of Napoleon and I have met others who try real hard to not bring their shit home with them. I have been arrested by the Napoleon types and by the cool ones, and there is a distinct difference. Now it is not beyond the realms of possibility that they reacted to me in one way or the other because I was either cool or a complete a-hole; but either way, the end result was on their terms, not mine.

Cops are an interesting group of people. If you can find a way to be respectful even though you are really thinking, "God, I wish he didn't have a gun. I would like to bust his face in," then in most cases, you will get treated in kind. If you are shit-faced and cop an attitude with a cop, he will cop an attitude right back at you and you will cop a nightstick upside the head real quick. Great, got *cop* in four times in one sentence.

If somehow, in that fuzzy alcohol-laden brain of yours, you can find a way to say sorry for being such a mess and that you will catch a taxi straight home, you might get lucky—but we all know that never happens as you will invariably say shit like the following:

1. "I have only had a couple of beers, Officer."
2. "I am not drunk. I puked because of something I ate."
3. "I was not going to drive. I was going to take a nap."
4. "I was not speeding. That was the car in front of me."
5. And, "Yes, I heard your siren and I know I didn't stop, but you see my wife recently ran off with a cop and I thought you were trying to bring her back."

Anyway, the point is that they do have guns, sticks, and lots of friends, and they can even throw in a German Shepherd or two as well, so don't fuck with 'em.

Unlike me when after a night out in Mayport Florida I managed to hook up with a young lady and have a session with her—yes that kind of session.

Two days later while in the same nightclub this guy comes at me with a pitcher with every intent to rearrange my face. It would seem that he was a little upset that I had fucked his missus a few nights earlier. Well after clipping him a few times, it all calmed down and we were escorted out of the premises (The top of the Holiday Inn), well my assailant, yes I am the victim here, is waiting outside so once again after a well aimed eight ouncer it is all over and done with—NOT. Stupid me turns to see a cop running at me full bore and instead of the smart approach I clip him, a good one as well. Needless to say, guns, nightsticks were all bought into play and after a bit of a hiding I was whisked off to jail. So do not fuck with the cops because you will not be as lucky as me. While I was collecting my stuff I noticed that a "Snoopy" pin that I had bought for a charity the night before was missing. I insisted that this cute Florida Policewoman find it, and after stating that she thought I was crazy, she did find it stuck in the bottom of the envelope. "Thank you" says I, and "what are you doing tonight"—the rest is smiley faces all around.

Except of course for 30 days on punishment when we left Florida—ces't la vie.

Finally, if you do need them, lawyers and or cops, do not hesitate to call them if someone is dicking around with you, don't try to take care of it yourself. Get it on paper so that when you do decide to give some butthead a smack in the nose, there is documented evidence that you tried to get help but this person did not back off. Seven years ago, I had an issue with a neighbor who would not control his pit bulls. Eventually, I ended up flattening him, and while I did not get into a lot of trouble, there was no documentation to my problem, so he got the benefit of the doubt. Next time around, someone was making "gun motions" toward my dog from his house. I immediately called the Sheriff, and boy, did his sphincter tighten up. Just remember, it is better to have them on your side rather than not because if they arrest you, it can go to the next group (see below) who can be real A-holes as well.

DA's and attorneys—you cannot deal with one without dealing with the other. It is a lose-lose situation for you as you have to pay your lawyer to fight their system and for the most part you will lose and end up paying both ends.

DA's do an amazing job for us even though it may not feel like it when you fuck up. Take your shit like a man and be all "Yes sir, no sir, three bags full, sir." Get on their wrong side and look the fuck out. Remember this about DAs—they get paid shit to do what they do, and they work ungodly hours. Making their lives harder will, in all likelihood, give them a perverse sense of enjoyment, and they will come up with creative ways to give it right back.

As to the other type of lawyers, well, they can be good and bad as well. Bottom line is they can all sprout the same shit and charge you the same money so if you get in trouble, get the one with the relationships within the court system. Do not get your buddy to represent you for free if he does not spend every waking minute in your courthouse of choice. He will get fucked off and told to go on his merry way, and you will get hammered.

Last but not least remember this; even if you do not remember another thing in this book. Outside of the good old US of A, you have *no fucking rights—none.*

Was that clear enough—*none*—especially in that shit hole to the south of us. In Mexico, you will go to jail unless you can bribe some Federale to take your money and let you go. No money and you are going to jail and forget the "Hey there, where is my phone call?" bullshit. You stay there until your drunk buddies notice that you are missing. In Mexico, you better see my earlier chapter and learn to be a big dog real quick—for the most part, your cell mates won't fuck with you, but if they get an inkling they can, then you better be real aggressive either verbally or physically.

You shouldn't get killed down there unlike many other world countries. But once again, when abroad, realize that your American passport doesn't mean shit. In Tunisia, they will find you dead behind the jail. In Columbia, they will give you up for ransom. In Brazil, you will give them everything and even drive them to your hotel room to empty that as well. So if you go and get fucked up somewhere, make sure you are surrounded by like-colored people, make sure that you are not alone, and, sure as fuck, make sure that you have the "where it all" to get out of any situation you are in. I have personally ignored everything I just said and am still here—you might not be so lucky.

CHAPTER 7

ILLEGAL DRUGS

Since it is two words, how about a quick overview.

Some illegal drugs are hallucinogens (drugs that make you see things that are not real, kind of like twenty beers). Cannabis (the official name of marijuana) used to be sold in coffee shops. The more powerful word for marijuana is Hashish. Another popular drug is Cocaine. Cocaine is oil found in leaves in a South American plant. This drug is very addictive—no shit. Heroin was considered a morphine in 1874. Heroine is a white powder with a bitter taste. A single dose of heroine is about one hundred milligrams. PCP (Phencyclidine) was invented in the 1950s. This product was originally made to be an anesthetic, but the patients became easily angered and delusional, so it was kicked off the market. The most common street names for this drug are Angel Dust, Ozone, Wack, and Rocket Fuel. Steroids are substances related to male sex hormones. Steroids are most commonly used by athletes to become bigger and stronger and to die young.

LSD (lysergic acid diethylamide) is a major drug in the hallucinogen class. LSD was found in 1938; this is the greatest mood-changing drug. LSD is a fungus that grows on grains.

Okay, so I just cut and pasted this info and is about as close to research as I think I can get. The reason is I know fuck all about real drugs. Well, drugs in general because they are all real, just that the big real nasty ones I have never touched. Kind of interesting really that of all the stupid shit I have done in my life, not once ever have I done crack, heroin, or cocaine. Now that leaves other things, and yes, I have dabbled, but I would hardly call myself a drug user. Except Viagra—yeah, baby.

Let me start by saying this: don't do drugs—ever. There is *no* upside for taking illegal drugs, none. I have known three people who died from drug overdose, and that is three too many.

My limited exposure to drugs first started in Cardiff Wales, where some bright spark introduced me to the world of magic mushrooms. Holy shit, I was in so much pain the next day because I laughed so hard for approximately three hours nonstop.

Now I did not see little green men like one friend, and I did not feel the need to shit in Dessie's hat like one of the others. But there was not one thing that could have happened that would not set me off in fits of laughter, painful rib-splitting laughter and milk-from-your-nose type of giggles. I swear my testicles could have fallen off and rolled across the floor and been squashed by some fat bastard sitting at the bar and I would have thought that was the funniest thing that could have possibly happened.

My second time with the mushrooms was at a Christmas party sometime around 1992/1993—ate the mushrooms and nothing—until I ended up showing my mate a picture of my dog and he commented that I should have the picture blown up. My magic mushroom response was, "I love my dog. Why would I blow him up?" and that was it. Two hours of blown-up dog jokes and nonstop laughing. So on the mushroom front, about three times total that I can remember.

Now to the "marajewana"—approximately 1991 was the first time, and maybe only three times since. Twice at Jimmy Buffett's concerts when someone passed me a joint and I took a puff and passed it on.

I never really noticed much of anything at the time as I was too fucked up on margaritas and shots of tookillya to really notice. The next time was Chicago. Playing golf while it was pissing down with rain, lightning everywhere, and I am running down the fairway with my seven iron high in the air, shouting, "Go on, I fucking dare you." Trying to get hit by lightning seemed to be funny as fuck at the time, as it is now, but only because I didn't get zapped.

All in all, nothing too harmful, and for sure, no arrests, etc. But like I said, there is no upside to taking illegal drugs. As I have been known to say, "I am a stupid fucker on beer. Why do I need drugs to make me any dumber?" I have seen firsthand the destructiveness of drug abuse, and it is not pretty. There is a reason they are illegal, and that is because they destroy the lives of the users and everyone around them. Like I said, I don't know much about them, but I know enough to never get serious with them.

CHAPTER 8

RELIGION

re li gion

noun

Date: Who cares

1. a set of beliefs concerning the cause, nature, and purpose of the universe, esp. when considered as the creation of a superhuman agency or agencies, usually involving devotional and ritual observances, and often containing a moral code governing the conduct of human affairs.
2. a specific fundamental set of beliefs and practices generally agreed upon by a number of persons or sects: *the Christian religion; the Buddhist religion.*
3. the body of persons adhering to a particular set of beliefs and practices: *a world council of religions.*
4. the life or state of a monk, nun, etc.: *to enter religion.*
5. the practice of religious beliefs; ritual observance of faith.
6. something one believes in and follows devotedly; a point or matter of ethics or conscience: *to make a religion of fighting prejudice.*

Now this one is going to be fun and piss off a fair chunk of people.

Let me start by saying this—I do not hold that some little black fucker with a bone through his nose in the middle of the rain forest is any less religious for worshiping a piece of wood than some pious motherfucker who worships Jesus Christ once a week. If that piece of wood gives him the sustenance to determine right from wrong and how to treat his fellow man, then good for him.

So if you can't tell by now, I am not a big fan of organized religion. I do believe that there is a greater power, but I refuse to recognize him/her/it by name.

Religion has fucked up this world more than anything that we can imagine. Just about every war had a religious crusade of some kind associated with it. Just about every conflict is some religious group trying to convert another religious group to their way of thinking. Personally, I believe that over the centuries, the Catholics were the worst.

They slaughtered millions in the name of religion, and the Protestants were not far behind. Whole civilizations where wiped out because they resisted being told who to worship and pray to.

I have the utmost respect for people of faith who do what they can to help the less fortunate. But at the same time, I hate with a passion those pious fuckers who will go out on a Saturday night, get fucked up, do drugs, harpoon a fat chick, clean up nice and pretty, and go to church the next morning and pray for forgiveness. Religion should be a guideline for right and wrong, nothing else; and if you need Jesus, Mary, Buddha, the Dalai Lama, or anything else to tell you which is which, then you need more help than holding your hands up.

For example, I am often asked about the Northern Ireland conflict, and I come up with the same response every time—a minority group (the Catholics) wanted to take over and change the will of the majority (the Protestants) who wanted to stay under British rule.

The Catholics had all the weaponry; hence, the need for the British army to police the colony. Sounds simple, doesn't it? But it is not so simple. Both sides, Catholics and Protestants, during the "troubles" were ruthless, vicious bastards who used religion to justify their actions. Either side would think nothing of kneecapping someone for having sex with a person of the opposing religion. Kneecapping is a lovely work of art where someone will either hammer a nail through your kneecap or if there is an abundance of bullet they will shoot you through the kneecaps.

Shit, you could have been killed for marrying outside of your religious group, and adultery or fucking a married woman was guaranteed to bring some serious shit on your head. The point is each side disagreed on a religious basis, and neither church would, at that time, work for a compromise. Now thank he/she/it who cannot be named, they finally worked it out—way too many people died before they could do so and in the Good Book which both sides read where the fuck does it say it's okay to blow up women and children?

Bosnia, Africa, Tibet, Russia, Northern Ireland, India/Pakistan, the Crusades, the Spanish Inquisition, and on and on. All little gems in the name of religion. Me, personally, I go to church for weddings or funerals, and that is it. I am disgusted that the Catholic Church and the priesthood got away with child molestation for so long. Not that they were unique, it nearly happened to me at a Church of England hell hole when I was young.

Where in the world can a child molester have numerous people come forward and tell the powers that be that they were molested and the only penalty for the molesters is to get moved to another church so they could do it again?

Oh, and to have the church buy off the victims, give me a fucking break—those priests should have been hung from the rafters and their victims should have been allowed to piñata their asses with baseball bats.

As to the amount of money they spend on themselves, some of these new churches are sick. Millions and millions of dollars to build, but the homeless shelter down the road had to close because their budget of $25,000 for the year got cut. Fucking hypocrites—want to help people? then make the church into a big ass homeless shelter and put it to good use outside of Sunday mornings and wedding and funerals.

Okay, on a roll now, are people really that fucking stupid that they believe that someone can turn water into wine, that someone was raised from the dead, or that some preacher with a really bad hairdo can touch them and heal their illnesses. I guess they must be because tens of thousands of people pack those churches and give them money they can ill afford no matter how many times those pious crooks fuck up and get caught stealing, fucking the secretary, or playing with the choir boys. Of all our domestic religions, the Mormon one seems to be the most consistent. The ones I know seem to hold their religion very dear and seem to be scarily nice.

Me, wouldn't touch their religion with a barge pole. I can barely handle having one wife, let alone many; and to have more than one wife and not be allowed to drink heavily would be suicidal. And giving up 10 percent of what I make—fuck that. Religion in general can shove it.

Don't preach to me. I know the difference between right and wrong, and I do not need some dickhead with bad hair and dimples to tell me which is which. And if all those people who think that someone can push you in the face and cure dementia, well, I have a big tower in France for sale. My favorite is the door-to-door religious nuts. Thankfully, not so many now, but, boy, it was good to fuck with them:

"Good day to you son of Christ—have you spoken to Jesus today?"

"Actually, yes, but my neighbor's wife came over to get laid before her husband got home, and I was in the middle of fucking her in the ass before you rudely interrupted."

Or, "No, sorry, I was busy trying to cut the three sixes out of my sons scalp before his mother got home."

Or, "Fuck off before I set my dog on you."

All in all, religion sucks. Just do the right thing or take an approach that if you wouldn't want something to happen to you, then don't do it to someone else and you'll be fine. Oh, wanna know why I am so anti-organized religion, no? Tough shit. It's because the orphanage that I grew up in made us go to church at least six times a week—couldn't read anything outside of the Bible or watch any raunchier than PG *minus* fucking ten shows on the TV. No wonder I ran away every chance I got.

Okay, I guess I need to go and confess my sins now. Gonna take a tent and some supplies because I will be there for a while and gonna need some serious medicinal help as I am sure to break out in hives or some shit. Of course that is assuming I don't get struck by lightning the second I walk in the door.

CHAPTER 9

GIRLFRIENDS

girl-friend

Noun:

Date: 1855-1860—fuck that, we have always had girlfriends otherwise we wouldn't be here since a-sexuality is not YET a human trait—stupid dictionary

1. a frequent or favorite female companion; sweetheart
2. a female friend
3. a species who can and will make your life miserable, and great, all in one foul swoop

---

Just decided to add this at the last minute, pissed off the editor, when I heard someone talking about a book about how to keep your boyfriend "in tow" yes "in tow". So I thought why not tell the boys how to keep their girlfriends in line and maybe find the right one while you are still young enough to get it up without Viagra.

Over the years I have had many girlfriends though I wouldn't necessarily call them girlfriends. I would more likely call them shagging partners as outside of the sex there was not a lot of camaraderie to speak of—see bootie call section. But over the years I have had what I would call four great loves.

The first one is always the one that you remember, the one you see and the second you do you go "wow, that is who I want to marry". Now that very rarely happens because once you get to know her you might find out she is a raging psycho but if you can strike up a relationship with that "first love" you will both learn, in depth, what it will take to make it long lasting and meaningful and even if it doesn't work out you will get some good intel.

Mine was D. who worked in the local café and everyone with testicles chased her incessantly. She had a lovely, no makeup and zit free face with very long beautiful hair and big tits. I decided she was going to be my girlfriend and I made it my mission to get her to go out with the quiet young man in the corner. You see that was my tactic, while everyone else was being loud and obnoxious in the café, I was quiet and thoughtful which confused the fuck out of my friends because I was certainly not quiet or thoughtful. I used to pay for my breakfast and buy a candy bar break half off and leave it on the counter for her. Okay stop gagging you insensitive bastards. I had no money, hadn't learned the gift of the gab yet so I improvised and before you choke that tactic worked very well for me over the years so fuck off. After a while I would find myself waiting after the lads left "I'll catch you up in a minute".

After cleaning my table 40 times per shift I finally asked her to come to the arcade on the pier with me and that was it.

Never got into her undies, she was only sixteen, but we snogged until our lips were numb and what happened to her mammary's, is between me and my memories.

I was only stationed there 6 months so after I moved away that was it because by now shagging was my primary reason for living. I saw her once many years later and the spark wasn't there though she still looked great and I could have sworn her tits had got bigger. The nice thing about D. was that we didn't fight, it was good old fashioned romance and it was great that neither one of us had learned how to be cynical, conniving or mean to each other.

Don't worry that soon changed as I got older.

Over the following years many girlfriends came and went, most came—get it? Some I should have or could have settled down with, some I should just enjoyed while I could and some I should have told to fuck off the day I met them.

Looking back I think the one thing that I would have loved to teach the younger me would have been "be yourself".

Over the years you will try to adapt yourself to the chickadee who's pants you are trying to get into and that can be a huge mistake. Your genes are your genes and I know that this is not scientific but that is what makes you unique and staying true to who you are (fuck I sound like Paula Abdul, talking of nice tits) is a sound direction.

I had this girlfriend once, drop dead beautiful, restaurants would go silent when she walked in, she could fuck like a jack rabbit but between the two of us, apart from the sex, we could barely function. Two way street—she had baggage from a boyfriend in bum fuck Arkinsaw (piss off that is how it sounds and how I am going to spell it) and I was awed by her looks and the sex. In hindsight I should have gone back to the fat chicks who appreciated a good rogering without a bunch of bullshit. This one nearly put me in the grave and totally took control of my cognitive thinking as in I was a blithering idiot with every smile. I would wait by the phone, sit outside her house, go by where she worked and everything that your big brain tells you you shouldn't do. What you should do is say "fuck you, I change my shorts in public after a rugby game, I don't have the money to pay for your dinner and fuck you so what if I have a crappy piece of shit car. If you don't like it fuck off back to your redneck loser and leave me alone".

Of course that didn't happen and it wasn't until I moved away that I finally got my head back on straight.

The point is you need to be yourself and not change too dramatically to fit what YOUR vision is of what a particular cutie wants you to be.

The woman you want to keep is the one who likes you just the way you are whether you are a foul mouthed, hard drinking dumbass or a church going goody two shoes. A good women is the one who will see the upside of being patient with you on day one and who is willing to invest the time to change you slowly but surely to someone she can put up with. Come to terms with the fact you will change and that if she is Miss Right it will worth it in the long run and things will work out.

Now the same applies to you. Don't try to change your girlfriend. I know most of us are lazy fucks and we won't invest too much time in trying to change them to our way of thinking unless of course it is how good anal sex is. But, you should allow a keeper to work slowly on changing you and between the pair of you both will change to a point where you can stay in a long term relationship.

Looking back there is nothing very funny about previous relationships once they end. Of course there were good times during the relationships but the end is rarely good. I had this one girl that I really liked and the sex was amazing and we did it each and every way in each and every place we could even in the women's rest room at a 5 star hotel with me speaking in a high pitched voice to some fat cow who wanted to take a shit. "I'll be right out just changing my tampon" I shout through the door because my girlfriend had a mouthful, damn if she didn't nearly bite my dick off she laughed so hard. We just got out of there as security came around the corner. Good times can cancel out bad.

Each and every relationship is going to be different and I am for sure not going to tell you to treat each girl you meet like a princess because some like that and some don't. There is a lot to be said about treat them like shit, no I don't mean abuse them, I mean stand them up every now and then, go out with the boys when you want, come home absolutely shit faced on occasion and of course that pig favorite, come in their hair. The key is that you need to recognize which ones want to be treated like princesses and which ones want to be treated like whores and YOU decide, not them, how much effort you are prepared to put in to make it work. If zero effort then find that slut who is fun to hang with, drinks like a fish and fucks like a trooper.

If you are thinking long term clean up your act, not too much, and be prepared to put in the appropriate amount of effort to keep her happy. I went thru a period of saying "fuck'em if they don't like it, I will find someone who does" and that seemed to work really well until I met someone who seemed to want to invest a considerable amount of time to save my miserable soul. There is a lot to be said to "love'em and leave'em" but you cannot do that indefinitely.

You will work out that sometimes the chase is better than the kill. I once chased this girl for nigh on four years. I turned into a masturbating machine if she so much as looked at me. After making the grade with some elite "you had better be fit" type unit and thickening up somewhat she started paying some attention to me and I finally ended up bagging her. Holy crap what a lousy fuck, I have had better sex with a battery powered vagina in an observation hide in the woods. The only good thing that came out of that episode was that my best mate (god bless him) back door'd me (that means he fucked her without my permission) when I went away on a course and thank him who cannot be mentioned but they hit it off. I often say that is because he was as lousy a fuck as she was. But I guess we will never know as men don't discuss their sexual prowess we all assume that we are all studs. Thanks Buddy.

All in all you cannot survive without women, unless of course you are gay and even they have their fag hags. You just definitely need to realize early on it life that it is a rough road that you will be travelling. Personally I feel that mine was like negotiating a volcanic lava field. If yours can be closer to a rough patch of dirt you are well ahead of the game.

CHAPTER 10

RACISM

rac-ism

noun

Date: 1865-1870—really, since the beginning of time as some poor bastard has been discriminated against in some form or another forever . . .a belief or doctrine that differences among the various human races determine cultural or individual achievement usually involving the idea that one's own race is superior and has the right to rule others. A policy, system of government, etc., based upon or fostering such a doctrine; discrimination. Hatred or intolerance of another race or other races.

You know what a pussy I am. I actually thought about taking this chapter out; then I thought to myself, Why should I? How many of us black, white, yellow, or green skinned people sit around debating, bitching, or just flat out solving the world's racial problems and do nothing about it. Outside of our drunk group of friends who, due to racism, are for the most part the same color as us, we never get to voice what we feel as being a valid opinion. Well, fuck it—I am typing this. I am paying to get this shit published and by fuck I am going to vent even if it is for my own gratification.

I will state in my dying declaration that this book needs to be shot into space so Aliens can really understand how fucked up the human race is. By the way, this might negate my "smaller chapters" comment earlier.

Okay, where to start. We are all racist—yes, every fucking one of us, but not according to the rest of the world, according to everyone else the only racists in the world are white.

What!!!!

Well think about it . . .

There are African Americans, Mexican Americans, Asian Americans, Muslim Americans, Arab Americans, etc. and then there are just Americans. I have been called White boy, snowflake, Cracker, Honkey, Whitey, Caveman and I am not allowed to get all incensed that I am being discriminated against, but "he who cannot be named" help me if I whisper the words Nigger, Kike, Towel head, Sand-nigger, Camel Jockey, Beaner, Gook, or Chink I am now a fully badged racist.

Non-whites say that whites commit a lot of violence against minorities but come on. Run the numbers, most of the violence in the US is within similar racial segments.

Minorities spew their anti racist rants every time a white commits a crime against a non white but when a black kills another black in a drive by it is NOT racism. If a black walked thru my town no one would shoot him in the face even though we are all obviously racists but look the fuck out if I strolled into South/East LA I would be fucked up or dead so quickly that passer bys wouldn't even break stride. But that is not racism, that is WHAT???

There is the United Negro College Fund, Black History Month, Yom Hashoah, Ma'uled Al-Nabi. There is the NAACP and BET (Black Entertainment TV) and the Black America

Pageant (not a Hispanic one yet thank fuck—short fat mamasitas in their bikinis not a pretty sight). See that would be racist from me but not if some non white said "better than seeing those skinny white ho's who are dumber than shit" . . .

If we had WET (White Entertainment Television), we'd be racists. If we had a White Pride Day, you would call us racists. If we had a WHITES only college it would be shut down as racist. If we had White History Month, we'd be racists. If we had a legal foundation directed to prosecute every non white who commits a crime against a white person—shit we would have tens of thousands of new lawyers (and no one wants that) who would all be racists—even the Black ones.

And finally if we had an organization to help whites "only" to advance their lives they would be racists. We have a Hispanic Chamber of Commerce, a Black Chamber of Commerce, and then we just have the plain Chamber of Commerce and guess who pays for that? All of us, But we cannot call it a White Chamber of Commerce.

If we had a college fund that only gave white students scholarships . . . . You know we'd be racists, yet there are over 60 openly proclaimed Black Colleges in the US. No 'White colleges' that would be too racist.

In the Million Man March, people believed that they were marching for their race and rights. If whites marched for their race and rights it would be a racist march. People are proud of their national and cultural heritage and that is encouraged, If whites show pride in being pink they are racists.

When in the wrong place at the wrong time we get robbed, car jacked, and shot at. But, when a white police officer shoots a gang member or beats up a drug dealer running from the law or someone who is beating his wife, they are racists. Trust me, this honky boy has received more than one good kicking from the men in blue but I did not call them pigs or racists just mother fuckers which is not a racial term unless you live in Tennessee.

Oh shit that is definitely racist or at least discriminatory.

So assuming that I have sufficiently pissed off a large group of indignant people who say "I am NOT a racist" . . . Let me clarify.

Us white folks do not have a monopoly on racism especially the younger generation who is paying on a daily basis for Bubba and His redneck buddies from the old days. I don't know a single person who has hung a black man, robbed a Mexican or beaten up a non white simply because they were not white. Sure we make black jokes my favorite is that "I was as drunk as a black Santa Claus on the Fourth of July" and some people might use the word nigger and spic and wetback, I don't, but how about the blacks and Hispanics? Since research was not a focus of this book, I would bet that people smarter than me can come up with a nice long list of racial epitaphs related to us pink folks.

If we can all agree that we are racists in some form or another I think we will come to terms with it a little easier than we do now.

By the way, just because you had a black friend growing up, it does not exempt you from being a racist. Just because there were a few Mexicans in your class in school does not mean you are not a racist.

Just because you fucked an Asian chick does not mean you are not racist. Lucky maybe, but a still racist. See that was a racist comment.

The thing is everyone has their own version of that comment—a big black guy will think nothing of rogering the shit out of a white girl—but taking her home to mum? No way, no how. This is the crux of the Rubik cube of life—you can mix it up, but when you finish the puzzle, all the sides are the same color.

If you want to pooh-pooh my "You are all racists" comment, then meet someone from the other side of the color spectrum. Take them out on a date and invite them to a party where all your black, yellow, white or brown homeboys are going to be, stick a big lip lock on them, take them home to meet Grandpa and then marry the bitch at a nice open bi-racial wedding and cap it off with some little half caste kiddy poos. For anyone who has been through that process, they are the purest of the pure—they went through hell to dispel any notion of racism and said, "Fuck you, I love this person no matter their color or race." Those people are few and far between—think about it.

The bullshit that is reverse racism just pisses me off. If whites said and did half of the shit some people do, the world would be up in arms.

Now I am not talking about some fucked-up redneck in the Mississippi delta. I am talking about you and me.

What about affirmative action. How many young white men and women have busted their asses to get a good GPA to get into college and have been fucked over and have to go to some community college because some minority motherfucker with a 3.0 GPA got their slot. Am I a racist for saying that or am I just pissed off? Racist according to Sharpton and Jackson.

Now let's talk about those two racist fuckers. If a white politician spilled a fraction of the bile that spills out of their mouths they would be run out of town. Being black does not give them the right to be racists. They routinely crucify the system and any white person who is involved in a crime against another race. Due process be damned. "I will pay for that poor black girl's college education." It didn't mean shit to them that she was a lying "wannabe hooker." They just couldn't pass up the chance to crucify some atypical white boy's. Of course they apologized and offered to pay the wrongly accursed/accused—not. They are the problem. Every time minorities crawl out the hole of inequality Jackson and Sharpton and Co. throw them back in with their anti establishment and racial equality rants.

They should leverage their ill gotten celebrity and focus on what black people do to other black people and not hang every white person who so much as sneezes germs in a black persons direction. I would bet every penny I could ever earn that for every Rodney King there is a Reginald Denny. Once again by example, Sharpton and Jackson by their very reaction and hate filled rhetoric cost some people their lives and tens of millions of dollars by fueling the flames of hate after "that" court case. Yet Reginald Denny who was nearly murdered said he forgave Football Williams for clearly attempting to kill him for BEING WHITE. Am I only one who see's those two bigots as obstacles not solutions to racial equality.

Take sports—for fuck's sake why can't we say that blacks are better athletes, or that he is a big gorilla? In some cases they are. They are faster and in many cases, bigger and stronger. Are we supposed to call a massive white guy "a big Gorilla" and a massive black guy "a person of African descent who is 6 foot 5 with big muscles who can run the 40 in 4.4 seconds". Fuck that he is a big gorilla as well and that is not a racial slur. I have a huge white mate who is routinely called a "big fucking gorilla". Shit there is a black guy playing Rugby for South Africa as we speak whom they call the "Beast"—yes, the commentators and the crowd shout out "Beast" every time he touches the ball.

Is he pissed off? No he loves the love and recognition to his athletic ability. Sorry mate but Jackson and Sharpton will be on the next plane to put a stop to that little example of racism. Holy shit, can you imagine if Al Michaels said that number 45 was a beast. He would be out of a job so fast.

So am I a racist because I say black people can't swim worth shit? Yep, according to the politically correct world we live in. It doesn't matter that they can't swim worth shit. I'm a racist. But when a black guy says, "White men can't jump," oh fucking lordy, that's okay, because white guys can't jump. See my point?

There are some very fucked-up people on both sides of the coin, but for the record, I am more impressed by deed than word. Abe Lincoln, MLK, Nelson Mandela, Cesar Chavez, and every other "crusader", including many whites who died to promote racial equality. There was a great line in the movie Glory where Denzel Washington's character was denigrating some white troops who were retreating only to be slapped in face by Morgan Freeman's character who poignantly pointed out that "these white boys have been dying in their thousands and dying for you fool. I know 'cause I dug their graves". How soon we forget.

I once got into a little fisticuffs with some white racist skinheads just because the people they were beating on were black. Now some people can say I jumped in and knocked some heads to help the blacks out or that I did it because they were fucking scum bags picking on two people who were in the wrong place at the wrong time. Who cares. "Hey mate what are you doing? You one of us" . . .

As I gently explained to them with a head butt and a few well aimed punches and kicks "No I ain't and never will be" . . .

The point is every racial group has racists but it is unreasonable to tar "whites" as the only group of racists. I certainly wouldn't hold my breath waiting for a black man to come and save my ass in a bad neighborhood, much like no one helped Reginald Denny. People will whine no matter what but whining because of the color of their skin to get an advantage in life or to make an excuse because of their lot in life don't cut it. Sorry but I am white, had a shitty childhood, no money, no family, no education and I turned out "reasonably" well. Not once have I ever blamed my lot in life on being white or because of something done to me by another color and I sure as shit have had enough of getting blamed for the slave trade and the confederacy.

Okay, I know it's time to lighten the fuck back up so I will.

PS. Halle Berry is one hot Black Mama—watch Monters Ball.

CHAPTER 11

MANIFESTO

Just some quick baselines on how to keep you manhood intact at all times . . .

1: Under no circumstances may two men share an umbrella, unless it has the following printed on it: "if you bitches want to come under here then you had better put out".

2: It is OK for a man to cry ONLY under the following circumstances:
   (a) When a heroic dog dies to save its master
   (b) They show Joe Theisman's leg breaking
   (c) The moment Halle Berry starts unbuttoning her blouse
   (d) After wrecking your boss' car with him in it
   (e) One hour, 12 minutes, 37 seconds into "The Crying Game"
   (f) When she is using her teeth

3: Any Man who brings a camera to a bachelor party may be legally killed and eaten by his buddies.

4: Unless he murdered someone in your family, you must bail a friend out of jail within 12 hours.

5: If you've known a guy for more than 24 hours, his sister is off limits forever unless you actually marry her.

6: Moaning about the brand of free beer in a buddy's fridge is forbidden (UNLESS IT IS COORS LIGHT). However complain at will if the temperature is unsuitable or they run out.

7: No man shall ever be required to buy a birthday present for another man. In fact, even remembering your buddy's birthday is strictly optional. At that point, you must celebrate at a strip bar of birthday boy's choice.

8: On a road trip, the strongest bladder determines pit stops, not the weakest.

9: When stumbling upon other guys watching a sporting event, you may ask the score of the game in progress, who is losing big to the bookie but don't ask who's playing.

10: You may flatulate/fart/let rip in front of a woman only after you have brought her to climax at least once. If you trap her head under the covers for the purpose of "stinky" entertainment she's now officially your girlfriend.

11: It is permissible to drink a fruity alcohol drink only when you're sunning on a tropical beach . . . and it's delivered by a topless waitress, it's free, highly alcoholic and you are sure to puke later.

12: Only in situations of moral and/or physical peril are you allowed to kick another guy in the nuts.

13: Unless you're in prison, never fight naked.

14: Friends don't let friends wear Speedos. Ever. Issue closed. If you have to ask about Man Thongs I will personally fly to your location and fuck you up.

15: If a man's fly is down, that's his problem, you didn't see anything, unless it is hanging out and huge then it is okay to high five him and go get medical help to be able to compete effectively.

16: Women who claim they "love to watch sports" must be treated as spies until they demonstrate knowledge of the game, the ability to drink as much as the men and the innate ability to pile drive one of the boys into the ground when drunk.

17: A man in the company of a hot, suggestively dressed woman must remain sober enough to fuck and fight.

18: Never hesitate to reach for the last beer or the last slice of pizza, but not both, that's just flat out greedy.

19: If you compliment a guy on his six-pack, you'd better be talking about his choice of beer.

20: Never join your girlfriend or wife in discussing a buddy of yours and his sexual activities unless of course she is withholding sex until you respond—and then you had better fucking lie and lie well.

21: Never talk to a man in a bathroom unless you are on equal footing, as in, both urinating, both waiting in line, both are confident in the size of your manhood. For all other situations, an almost imperceptible nod is all the conversation you need.

22: Never allow a telephone conversation with a woman to go on longer than you are able to have active sex with her. Keep a stopwatch by the phone and hang up if necessary.

23: The morning after you and a girl who was formerly "just a friend" have carnal, drunken, multiple orifice sex and just because you are feeling weird and guilty about it is no reason for you to not roger the shit out her again before beginning the "what a big mistake that was" discussion.

24: It is acceptable for you to drive your chicks car as long as it is not pink, however it is not acceptable for her to drive yours, unless you are too fucked up to drive and she is picking you up from an all night—all day—all weekend drinking session.

25: Thou shall not buy a car in the colors of brown, pink, lime green, orange or sky blue, it shall not have seat covers, air freshener or some bitches voice telling you to "please put on your seatbelt". What it will have is an Electronic Anti Abba/Manilow/George Michael device that will give your testicles an electric shock every time one of their songs comes on the radio. You will have a toilet roll holder that has rolls of condoms prominently displayed on the dash. You will also have empty beer cans in the back, a bottle or two, some used condoms with a glob of Vaseline in for effect (clean out the "real used" ones you disgusting sick bastards) and make sure that there are disparaging stickers on your car attacking cops, women, homosexuals and minorities.

26: The girl who replies to your question "What do you want for Christmas?" with "If you loved me, you'd know what I want!" gets a Kegerator and a Beer Pong Table. End of story.

27: There is no reason for guys to watch Men's Ice Skating no I don't mean hockey fuckwit, or Men's Gymnastics. Ever. Women's is okay if you make a beer drinking game out of it on who can get the first beaver shot, what kind of sexual positions you could invent if your girlfriend would only bend like that or anything perverted enough to get you arrested when discussing that 16 year old with the hot bod.

28: Going grocery shopping with the missus is a big no no—unless and to be clear—you do not push the cart and you head straight for the beer, liquor, snacks, doughnuts and naughty magazine sections—oh and in case you have not figured this out yourself (what the fuck is the point of writing this if you haven't learned at least the basics) you also buy a pack of condoms and pay separately . . .

And finally we've all heard about people having guts or balls. But do you really know the difference between them? In an effort to keep you informed, the definition of each is listed below.

"GUTS" is arriving home late after a night out with the guys, being assaulted by your wife with a broom, and having the guts to say, "are you still cleaning or are you flying somewhere?"

"BALLS" is coming home late after a night out with the guys, smelling of perfume and beer, lipstick on your collar, slapping your wife on the ass and having the balls to say, "Come on Fatty you're next!"

FINAL CHAPTER

CLOSING POINTS OF VIEW/RANT

Okay, here we are. What started as a joke about three years ago has turned into a multipage rant made up of a bunch of funny and not-so-funny shit that has happened to me over the years.

Without being a pious bastard, I hope that you at least enjoyed reading it and that at least once you avoid some shit that you might have gotten into had you not read my sage words of advice.

I hope I make some money from this little book, anything would be great, oh bullshit, I would prefer a bucket load or have my own TV show or movie, but I'm not holding my breath and trust me I know I am not going to be on The Oprah Book Club Top Ten List.

My target audience is crazy young college kids who can maybe afford ten bucks for a good shit house read and hopefully *not* some crazy college kid who says, "Fuck him, I am going to view his book as a "how to" book and do everything he says not to do."

I think the bottom line is don't take life too seriously. You can be a grade A student and enjoy life or you can be a grade A student and be a miserable fuck. Of course, you can be a grade D student and really enjoy life and really not give a flying fuck. Me, I never graduated high school and I turned out just fine with a PhD in common sense that I would put against any diploma any day of the week. Of course, career and family come into it and I could have done a better job on that front; but you know what, if you can get to fifty years old and sit down and only have one or two really major regrets, you haven't done half bad.

When and if you do graduate from college, get the fuck out of dodge. Go travel for a while, watch the world go by, spend every penny you have, and enjoy life because trust me, once you get into the workplace, life as you know it is over.

No more partying every night of the week as you will have to put up with some dick head manager bright and early who is a lot worse than any teacher you ever had. You will invariably settle down so fucking everything in sight is no longer an option assuming of course that you were ever that lucky in the first place. Confidence, confidence, confidence.

Have the confidence to do whatever you want, when you want to do it.

Whether taking on the local bully, trying to fuck the hottest girl in town, applying for a job way out of your league, or telling your soon to be ex-boss to go fuck himself. Whatever it is, do it confidently.

I didn't do a section on friends because I want to keep the ones I have but I did want to touch on that in closing. If you have five friends in your life, consider yourself lucky. I am not talking about acquaintances, roommates, team buddies, drinking or fucking buddies; I am talking about real friends who would empty their bank account for you, go down fighting for you, or jump on the proverbial grenade (I mean fuck a fat chick so you can fuck the hot one) for you. Don't try to be the most popular person in the world—take care of your best friends and the world will follow along. And just remember, at least one of your friends is going to be a real a-hole, in my case it was me, but you know what he is your own personal a-hole, so look after him—he will need it—I did.

Can't really think of anything else even close to being meaningful, and even though this is a short book, I intentionally decided to not fill it with a bunch of fluff to make it thicker. Yeah, right! The truth is, I'm not smart enough to come up with any more shit, and I am too bored to write any more of this crap anyway.

So thanks for reading and hopefully paying something for the pleasure of doing so. If you illegally downloaded this, photocopied it, or gave it to your buddy without exchanging it for beer or a blow job from "his" girlfriend then fuck you.

Stay safe.

RHE

INDEX

www.ingramcontent.com/pod-product-compliance
Lightning Source LLC
Chambersburg PA
CBHW031302280526
45784CB00004B/1959